SEYMOUR SIMON

WHALES

THOMAS Y. CROWELL NEW YORK

Whales

Copyright © 1989 by Seymour Simon

Printed in the U.S.A. All rights reserved.

Typography by Andrew Rhodes

1 2 3 4 5 6 7 8 9 10

First Edition

Library of Congress Cataloging-in-Publication Data

Simon, Seymour.

   Whales.

   Summary: Describes, in text and illustrations, the
physical characteristics, habits, and natural
environment of various species of whales.

   1. Whales—Juvenile literature. [1. Whales]
I. Title.

QL737.C4S495 1989   599.5'1   87-45285

ISBN 0-690-04756-8

ISBN 0-690-04758-4 (lib. bdg.)

Photo credits

Jacket front: Ocean Images, Inc./Al Giddings

Jacket back: Woods Hole Oceanographic Institution/
Karen E. Moore

pp. iv–v, 36, 38: Ocean Images, Inc./Al Giddings;

p. 12: Ocean Images, Inc./Rosemary Chastney;

pp. 7, 11, 14, 15, 17, 18, 20, 23, 28, 35, 40: Nicklin
& Associates/Flip Nicklin; pp. 8, 26, 31, 32: Woods
Hole Oceanographic Institution/Karen E. Moore;

p. 24: Woods Hole Oceanographic Institution/N. A.
Watkins

Photo on pp. iv-v: A group of humpbacks feeding.

In Noah's flood he despised Noah's Ark; and if ever the world is to be again flooded . . . then the eternal whale will still survive, and rearing upon the topmost crest of the equatorial flood, spout his frothed defiance to the skies.

—Herman Melville

Moby Dick, or The White Whale

The great whales are the world's giant animals. This humpback whale is breaching—jumping almost clear out of the water and then crashing down in a huge spray of foam. The humpback whale is longer than a big bus and heavier than a trailer truck. Some great whales are even larger. Just the tongue of a blue whale weighs as much as an elephant.

Whales are not fish, as some people mistakenly think. Fish are cold-blooded animals. This means their body temperature changes with their surroundings. Whales are mammals that live in the sea. Like cats, dogs, monkeys, and people, whales are warm-blooded. Their body temperature remains much the same—whether they swim in the icy waters of the Arctic or in warm tropical seas.

A fish breathes by taking in water and passing it through gills to extract oxygen, but a whale must surface to inhale air into its lungs. A whale's nostril, called a blowhole, is at the top of its head. A whale breathes through its blowhole. Some whales, such as the humpback, have two blowholes. Here they are open, as the humpback whale exhales old air and inhales fresh oxygen-rich air.

The air that whistles in and out of a whale's blowhole moves at speeds of two or three hundred miles an hour. It enters and leaves the lungs, within the whale's chest. With each breath, a whale inhales thousands of times more air than you do. The whale closes its blowhole and holds its breath when it dives. Some kinds of whales can dive to depths as great as a mile and hold their breath for more than an hour during a deep dive. When they surface, they blow out a huge breath and then take several smaller breaths before diving again.

A whale has a tail with horizontal flukes, which are different from the vertical tail fins of a fish. The fins of a fish have bones and move from side to side. Flukes have no bones and are moved up and down by powerful muscles connected to the whale's spine. The upward stroke of the tail pushes the whale through the water, sometimes at speeds of more than thirty miles per hour. From tip to tip, the flukes of a great whale are longer than a tall person.

A whale has forelimbs, with the same bones found in human arms. But over millions of years a whale's forelimbs have changed into flippers. The flippers help keep a whale's body steady and are used for steering and changing direction. Humpbacks have the longest and most flexible flippers of any whales.

The bones of a whale's skull form huge upper and lower jaws. Each tooth in this sperm whale's jaw weighs more than half a pound. Whales have no external ears, very little hair, and no sweat glands. A thick layer of fatty tissue beneath their skin, called blubber, helps insulate them against the cold water and also stores energy. Whales were once hunted mostly for their blubber, which was boiled down to whale oil aboard the whaling ships and used as fuel in oil lamps.

Like all other mammals, whales mate, and the females give birth to live young. The female, called a cow, usually has one baby at a time. A sperm whale cow carries her calf for as long as sixteen months, but most kinds of calves are born about a year after mating takes place.

A newly-born humpback whale calf is between twelve and fourteen feet in length. The mother humpback takes good care of her baby. At its birth, she pushes it to the surface so it can get its first gulp of air. A third whale often joins the cow and accompanies the mother and calf.

The mother squirts milk into the young calf's open mouth forty times a day. The milk is rich in fat and energy. Each feeding is very brief, because the baby must surface for air. But in a few seconds, the baby drinks two or three gallons of milk. In one day, a baby whale drinks more than 100 gallons of milk and may gain as much as 200 pounds.

A growing calf has much to learn. It practices diving, holding its breath, breaching, and other skills needed for its survival. When it is about seven months old, the calf stops nursing. It is now about twenty-five feet long and able to feed by itself.

There are about ninety kinds of whales in the world. Scientists divide them into two main groups: toothed whales and baleen whales.

Toothed whales have teeth and feed mostly on fish and squid. They have only one blowhole and are closely related to dolphins and porpoises.

The sperm whale is the only giant among the toothed whales. It is the animal that comes to mind when most people think of a whale. A sperm whale has a huge, squarish head, small eyes, and a thin lower jaw. All the fist-sized teeth, about fifty of them, are in the lower jaw. The male grows to sixty feet long and weighs as much as fifty tons. The female is smaller, reaching only forty feet and weighing less than twenty tons.

A sperm whale's main food is squid, which it catches and swallows whole. A sperm whale is not a very fast swimmer, but it is a champion diver. It dives to depths of a mile in search of giant squid and can stay underwater for more than an hour.

There are smaller and less familiar kinds of toothed whales. The narwhal is a leopard-spotted whale about fifteen feet long. It is sometimes called the unicorn whale, because the male narwhal has a single tusk. The tusk is actually a ten-foot-long front left tooth that grows through the upper lip and sticks straight out. No one knows for sure how the narwhal uses its tusk. Narwhals live along the edge of the sea ice in the Arctic.

Perhaps the best known of the toothed whales is the killer whale, or orca. That's because there are killer whales that perform in marine parks around the country. A killer whale is actually the largest member of the dolphin family. A male can grow to over thirty feet and weigh nine tons.

Orcas are found in all of the world's oceans, from the poles to the tropics. They hunt for food in herds called pods. Orcas eat fish, squid, and penguins, as well as seals, sea lions, and other sea mammals, including even the largest whales. Yet they are usually gentle in captivity, and there is no record that an orca has ever caused a human death.

Baleen whales differ from toothed whales. They have a two-part nostril or blowhole; and, instead of teeth, they have food-gathering baleen plates. Each whale has several hundred baleen plates, which hang down from the whale's upper jaw. The plates can be two to seven feet long and hang about one quarter of an inch apart. The inside edge of each plate is frayed and acts like a filter.

Baleen whales are the biggest whales of all, yet they feed on small fish and other very small sea animals, such as the shrimplike animals called krill. Krill, which are only as big as your little finger, occur in huge amounts in the Antarctic Ocean. In northern waters, baleen whales eat different kinds of small shrimplike animals.

Some baleen whales, such as the right whale, skim openmouthed through the water. The frayed inner edges of the baleen trap the food animals while the water pours out through the gaps. In this way a right whale can filter thousands of gallons of seawater and swallow two tons of food each day.

The right whale was once very common in the North Atlantic Ocean. It was given its name by early whalers who regarded it as the "right whale" to catch, because it swam slowly, had lots of baleen and blubber, and floated when dead. So many right whales were killed that they are now quite rare.

Right whales may reach more than fifty feet and weigh more than seventy tons. They have large flippers and a long lower lip that covers and protects their baleen plates. Each right whale has its own pattern of strange bumps along its head called callosities. Scientists sometimes identify individual whales by the patterns of their callosities.

The gray whale feeds differently from the way any other whale does. It swims on its side on the ocean bottom and pushes water out of its mouth between its baleen plates, stirring up sediment from the ocean floor. Then the whale draws back its tongue and sucks the sediment, and any living things around, into its mouth. As the whale rises to the surface, it rinses its mouth with fresh seawater and swallows the catch. This method of bottom feeding is sometimes called "grubbing."

Gray whales once swam, in both the North Atlantic and North Pacific oceans, in the shallow waters along the coasts. Now, because of whaling in the Atlantic, they live only in the North Pacific and Arctic seas.

In the summer, the gray whales feed in the cold waters of the Arctic. In the winter, they travel about ten thousand miles to Mexican waters. There, the females give birth in the warm, protected lagoons along the Baja California peninsula. The journey of the gray whales is the longest known yearly migration for any mammal.

With its long, streamlined body, its pointed head, and its thin flukes, the fin whale has the right shape to be a fast and nimble swimmer—and it is. The long grooves on its throat allow the throat to expand while the whale is feeding. Whales that have these grooves, such as the fin, minke, humpback, and blue, are called rorquals, from the Norwegian word for groove or furrow.

Fin whales often work in pairs to round up and eat schools of fish. Fin whales are second only to blue whales in size. They can reach seventy to nearly ninety feet in length and weigh eighty tons.

The minke whale is the smallest rorqual. Still, it is thirty feet long and weighs six to eight tons. Northern minke whales have a white patch across the top of each flipper. Southern-hemisphere minke whales lack this marking.

Minke whales are fast swimmers and can leap clear out of the water. Unlike many other whales, minkes will often approach and swim around ships at sea much the way dolphins do.

The blue whale is bigger than the largest dinosaur that ever lived. The largest known dinosaur may have been 100 feet long and weighed 100 tons. But the biggest blue whales are over 110 feet long and weigh more than 150 tons. That's the weight of twenty-five full-grown elephants. The heart of a blue whale is the size of a small car.

A blue whale swims along the surface of the ocean up to a cloud of krill, opens its mouth wide, and sucks in fifty or more tons of water in one gulp. Then it opens its lips and strains out the krill through its baleen plates. In one day a blue whale eats more than four tons of krill, about forty *million* of these animals.

Blue whales have been hunted for many years. Even though they are now protected, only small numbers of blue whales are found in the Antarctic or anywhere else in the world.

Humpback whales appear to be curious and seem to be accustomed to whale-watching boats. The whales show no hostility to the boats and are careful to avoid collisions.

Many whales make sounds, but the most famous are the songs of the humpbacks. They are sung only by the males. Some scientists think the songs may help to attract females or to keep other males from coming too close.

Whatever the reasons the whales have for singing them, the songs are strange and beautiful. Each one lasts as long as twenty or thirty minutes and is sung over and over again. The songs have patterns that repeat, but are different from one whale to another and from one year to the next. The song of a humpback can be heard from miles away.

Humpbacks feed in different ways. One way is called "bubble netting." A humpback sends out clouds of bubbles in a circle beneath a school of small fish or other food animals. When the fish are trapped by the bubbles, the whale lunges up inside the circle with its mouth open, swallowing huge amounts of water and food. A humpback's throat expands to make lots of room for the food and water. Sometimes several humpbacks feed together in the circle of bubbles.

In 1946, the International Whaling Commission (IWC) was set up to establish rules to limit whaling. Despite the rules, the numbers of whales steadily shrank. Some kinds of whales may be about to become extinct. Because of a worldwide movement to save the whales, the IWC banned all commercial whaling, beginning in 1985. But the governments of a few countries still allow their citizens to hunt whales.

Whales are one of the few wild animals that are commonly friendly to humans they encounter. Many people feel that we have an obligation to preserve these intelligent and special animals.

Will whales be allowed to remain to share the world with us? The choice is ours.